SUB SURVIV

A Handbook for the Substitute Elementary Teacher

Revised Edition

Danna O'Reilly Downing
Veteran Substitute Teacher

LEARNING PUBLICATIONS, INC.
Holmes Beach, Florida

Library of Congress Card Number: 80-83081

Learning Publications, Inc.
P.O. Box 1326
Holmes Beach, Florida 33509

ISBN 0-918452-85-6

Cover art and illustrations by Melinda Frink Kabel

Printing: 1 2 3 4 5 6 7 8   Year: 5 6 7 8
Printed and bound in the United States of America

ACKNOWLEDGMENTS

Although, by her request, only one name appears on this cover, Gisela VerHey deserves much credit for this publication. The workshop we developed together for the Kalamazoo Valley Intermediate School District is where it all began. Her enthusiasm and encouragement are a constant source of joy.

The ideas and observations embodied in this publication never would have been printed but for the many experiences and contacts I have had as a substitute teacher and workshop leader. I wish to thank *all* who have been a part of my professional and personal growth.

This book is dedicated to the memory of Robert Hughes for his role in initiating the project and also to my family for their support which faciliated its completion.

INTRODUCTION

Although Elementary Substitute Teachers have the same levels of enthusiasm and dedication as full time teachers, they must also learn how to survive the particular rigors of teaching in "the wilderness" without the comforts and security of their own classrooms. In addition, the "sub" often assumes the reduced status of "intruder" rather than "teacher."

This publication is designed especially for such "trail blazers" and will assist them to develop a personalized "survival kit." In addition, the text includes a large variety of classroom tested activities requiring minimal materials. These ideas were collected specifically to meet the needs of the substitute teacher's unpredictable and often challenging days in the classroom.

Underlying the text is a strong belief that substitute teaching can be a very rewarding experience when "subs" can enter the classroom with a sense of confidence knowing they are not only prepared but are also likely to leave behind a group of children who will remember the day as being very "special."

This publication has its roots in the experience of two substitute teachers: myself and my good friend, Gisela VerHey. Our approach to and enthusiasm for substitute teaching was a process of evolution.

Upon being requested to do an in-service presentation at our local intermediate school district, a crude SUB SURVIVAL HANDBOOK was designed to accompany the workshop. That little handbook and its ensuing revisions are the literary basis for this book. Preparation for that first workshop in 1974 also helped us to clarify and refine what we feel are definite advantages and successful strategies in substitute teaching.

An integral part of our preparation was a survey administered to the elementary teachers in a nearby school district. Approximately 100 teachers responded to the survey. Our basic approach to substitute teaching was strongly supported by the results of the survey.

Teachers were asked to rank a set of twelve statements in order of importance to them as they returned to their classrooms following an absence. Number "1" signifies the item teachers considered to be of greatest importance while number "12" signifies the item regarded to be of least importance.

1. My substitute has left a report which quickly brings me up to date in regards to what has occurred during my absence.

2. My sub made the day "special" for my students by adding his/her own creative touch.

3. My sub demonstrated skill in dealing with the emotional needs of my students.

4. My students demonstrated a positive reaction to my substitute when I returned.

5. My sub made an effort to become aware of and to follow school/classroom procedures and policies.

6. My substitute has used his or her own initiative in terms of planning and directing classroom activities.

7. My plans have been followed carefully.

8. Other teachers and observers report that my children were well behaved during my absence.

9. All papers, workbooks and assignments have been corrected.

10. All correspondence from parents, principal, etc., is located in one spot and labeled appropriately.

11. My desk is in order.

12. My sub has telephoned a report to me at the day's end.

Making the day "special" and one about which a substitute teacher can easily and proudly report is the intent of SUB SURVIVAL and is obviously valid in light of the teachers surveyed. Our perceptions and intuitions have been continually reinforced by each group of workshop participants. By examining their individual strengths and goals, they developed personalized survival skills so as to become successful substitute teachers.

You, too, will discover your potential for success and professional growth. I hope that SUB SURVIVAL will have been of some assistance in that process.

DOD

TABLE OF CONTENTS

BASIC SURVIVAL TIPS

Here are some "tried and true"

Basic Survival Tips

- Arrive at school as early as possible.

- Be sure to bring along your own "creature comforts," whatever they may be.

Don't depend on beverages, cups, etc. being available or on necessarily being able to find them.

- "Scout your new territory. Immediately locate or identify:

  1. Seating chart
  2. Plan book
  3. Class list
  4. Fire and safety drill procedures and exits
  5. Equipment and materials available for your use
  6. School floorplan showing: student bathrooms, library, cafeteria, faculty lounge and other critical "landmarks"

- Take advantage of any early arrivals. These "natives" are an excellent source of information.

- Take a few seconds to learn several names from the class list so that you will be able to enlist these people *by name* to do small chores. The children will be pleased to discover that you "know" their names. This helps to establish good rapport immediately.

- Name tags, desk markers, get-acquainted activities, or any other system which personalizes your relationship with the students and which holds an individual accountable in terms of behavior is to your immediate advantage.

- Providing you are comfortable in so doing, share parts of yourself with the class. It helps them to recognize you as a person in your own right -- not "just a sub."

- Let the class begin the day as they normally would (pledge, attendance, sharing, etc.) to create a "business as usual" climate. During this ritual you may gain considerable insight about group dynamics as well as potential resources and hazards.

- Initiate your part of the day with an interesting activity of your own creation. Such action is often a very useful technique for generating enthusiasm for the rest of the day.

- A rough outline of what's planned for the day written on the chalkboard will give the group (including you) a sense of direction. Special classes, lunch and dismissal times, as well as options and consequences, should be included in the outline.

- Keep explanations short and sweet.

- Bring along your own "survival kit" to compensate for poor "trail markers" incomplete, inadequate, or even invisible lesson plans! The majority of this book is devoted to suggestions for designing your own personal "survival kit."

- When appropriate, let the children correct their own work. It can be a learning process in itself and also provides valuable assistance to the "sub" whose time is usually very limited.

- Prepare a class list to be used for recording student participation throughout the day. If blank forms are always kept in your "survival kit" an individual student could fill in the blanks for you from a class roster. Another method would be for the form to be circulated around the room allowing each student to "sign in."

Student Check List Date: NAMES	*Expectation*				COMMENTS

- Don't forget to check the teacher's mailbox at mid-day in case there are notices which need to be sent home with the students that day.

- Employ student help to maintain and enhance your "survival kit."

- "Be on the look-out" for new ideas to add to your "survival kit." Inclusion of such new ideas will also assist to maintain and enhance your degree of enthusiasm.

- Keep a small notebook for the purpose of recording the classrooms in which you have substituted. Such a record may include notations pertinent to future work with the class and will also serve as some verification of your subbing experience as it relates to teacher certification requirements in your particular state.

- Leave the classroom in good order. Whenever possible, involve students in that process. The end-of-the day clean up chaos can often take its toll on a substitute teacher -- the final blow! A "Job Card" system can enable you to avoid many clean-up time pitfalls!

   Number a set of index cards from 1-35. On each card list one basic clean up task which would be appropriate in any classroom.

#1

Please erase all the chalkboards.

#2

Please straighten the desk arrangement.

Once you have exhausted these possibilities, create some open-index cards which would also be appropriate in any classroom.

One student should receive a "Person-in-Charge" card indicating his or her responsibility to do the initial check up on completed tasks.

The higher the number on the card, the lower the priority of the task.

This arrangement allows for classes less than 36 students.

Illustrations on each card make them more attractive and assist the non-reader.

The Job Cards are distributed to class members about 15 minutes prior to dismissal.

The children are instructed to do the task, get their coats, and then return to their desks. When everyone is quietly in their seats, the substitute begins to call numbers from 1-35. When the number is called, the child brings up the card and may line up for dismissal. As the children line up, the substitute and student person-in-charge can quickly check to see that the assigned task has been completed to their satisfaction. Not only do students depart in an orderly fashion -- the substitute does not have to spend his or her limited time on custodial matters. Such advantages are why Job Cards are a permanent part of many a substitute's "basic survival kit."

- Be sure to leave some sort of written report. Highlight any information pertinent to the next day's activities. Including your name and phone number can often be helpful and may serve to enhance your chances for being called again.

Dear   Date:

Following is a short report of our activities during your absence:
   ABSENCES:

   SPECIAL MESSAGES:

   FRIENDS WHO WERE GOOD HELPERS:

   AREAS OF DIFFICULTY:

MATH	READING
LANGUAGE ARTS	SOCIAL SCIENCE
SCIENCE & HEALTH	OTHER

COMMENTS:

"CRITTER CONTROL"

"Critter Control" in the "wilderness" is critical. Substitute teachers have been known to actually have nightmares about potential "beastly" students. Occasionally a substitute will encounter figments of those nightmares in the real flesh. But for the most part, any substitute teacher can effectively maintain discipline.

There is no one formula for effective discipline. What works for one substitute teacher may not work for another. What works in one classroom may not work in every classroom. But there are some basic ingredients in successful "critter control" which you may wish to consider.

- Arriving early and well prepared for the day helps to augment your "in charge" posture which students will respect.

- It seems imperative to quickly identify as many students by name as is possible. This establishes some early accountability for student behavior. Knowing names also personalizes the relationship you will have with your students.

- Like wild animals, many students will regard you as an intruder but will not attack if approached in a firm, warm, positive manner. Being too defensive or authoritarian seems to bring out the worst in a new group.

- It also seems important to make students aware that since you are an individual in your own right, who is temporarily acting in their regular teacher's place, the day may be a little different from usual but not necessarily less productive or less pleasant.

- Focusing in on the positive aspects of supportive cooperation from students seems to insure best results. Instead of marking down the names of troublesome students, make it clear you are looking for and reporting the names of helpful, cooperative, hard working students. Potential troublesome students should quickly be enlisted as helpers so as to convert them toward a successful day.

- If it is emphasized to the students that the responsibility for the day's success is shared by both them as students *and* you as the substitute teacher, it puts you all on the same team.

- Make your expectations for classroom behavior clear from the very start.

- Make the class also aware that the group has options for which there are related consequences. If students opt to be responsible and cooperative this behavior will result in being able to easily complete required work allowing time for more creative and rewarding activities.

- "Baiting the trap," so to speak, is often necessary for survival in the "wilderness" and such a technique for substitute teachers will often result in students who "eat out of your hand." A special indoor or outdoor recess (simple) or a special art activity (more preparation but still not too difficult) are examples of "bait" which are likely to motivate expedient execution of mandatory business. Such rewards can be dispensed to individuals as they complete requirements and have free time or can be given to the total class when all class members have met their individual requirements. Without such a "lure," routine tasks can be an all day affair and a source of great frustration for all involved.

It is true that there are no guarantees in terms of discipline when you are a substitute teacher because you lack some resources which the regular classroom teacher possesses such as parental involvement. But on the other hand you have novelty and the element of surprise in your favor. The incorporation of your own *honest* and *positive* approaches to the problem are your greatest asset and will usually bring about very successful "critter control."

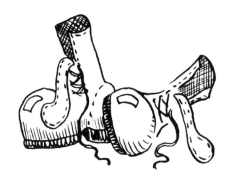

BASIC SURVIVAL KIT

Why a Survival Kit?

As a substitute teacher your odds for survival are based to a large extent upon "being prepared for anything!" Having your own personal "survival kit" is important in at least four ways:

1. Knowing you are "ready for anything" is a great boost to your confidence. A substitute's high level of confidence in turn elicits greater feelings of security and respect from students.

2. Bringing your own materials and supplies makes a substitute teacher relatively self reliant. It saves not only time but also prevents the classroom chaos which can erupt when the substitute teacher must "dig" for materials thereby sacrificing control over the group and/or the day's events.

3. A "survival kit" reflects the substitute's level of commitment to the day and the students; which is impressive to both students and potential employers.

4. The time spent in designing a "survival kit" not only improves your subbing experiences but also results in an end product which is readily adaptable to other professional and personal needs.

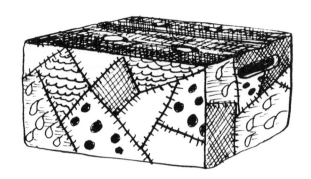

The Container Itself

The actual container is very important. It needs to be adequate in size, sturdy, transportable, and attractive. An empty beer case, for example, meets the necessary qualifications. The container itself may serve as a teaching tool that stimulates discussion, reveals the "true you," or provides fun, information or a challenge.

The possibilities for covering the container are virtually unlimited. Several possibilities include:

- Collage of magazine pictures showing the substitute teacher's hobbies, pets, family, travels, favorite foods, special interests, etc.

- Decorating the box to resemble an object such as a schoolhouse, truck, dog house, barn, schoolbus, city block, etc.

- "Quilting" the box with wallpaper scraps.

- Covering the box with riddles or puzzles which are numbered. Corresponding solutions could be attached inside the lid.

- Attaching pictures which might serve as provocative story starters.

The final step in any decorating strategy would be preservation. A coat of shellac or decoupage finish would be suitable in some cases. The use of contac paper is another possibility.

Possible Survival Materials For Your Kit

Following is a list of items which should be considered for inclusion:

pencils and pens

18" ruler

crayons and crayon stubs

felt markers

note pad

diary (in which to log work days)

scissors

stapler/staples

glue and glue stick

a package of lunch bags

* 12-15 egg carton bottoms

counters (beans, poker chips, macaroni)

stamp pad

masking tape

scotch tape

set of plastic name tag holders

* food coloring, toothbrush, piece of screen

magazines

magnets

picture file

* ditto file

yarn (at least 2 skeins)

straws

paper cups

paper plates

roll of shelf paper

decks of cards

sticker collection

bottle caps

cookie cutters (seasonal)

stencils

index cards

needle & thread

length of rope

paint brushes

timer

small rewards

* creative cards

* similar/different collections

* blank books

* games-commercial & home made

favorite short stories, books

phonograph records

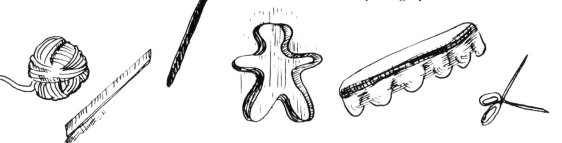

* further description and suggestions regarding these items can be found in the "Backpack Back-Up" section.

Key Criteria

Two key criteria for packing your "survival kit" are:

1. The "survival kit" should be personalized to meet individual needs. Because needs change, the contents may also change.

2. If space is limited it is perhaps important to include those items which could be used in many different ways rather than an item with limited possibilities.

Organization

There are limits to the sheer bulk any one substitute (who is not met at the door by an obliging custodian or principal) can carry into "the wilderness." For that reason careful packing is essential! Following are some suggestions for packaging and delivery systems which may prove helpful.

- Small and large Ziploc® plastic bags are ideal containers for many supplies or games. Such packages can be tucked into any little nook or cranny and the contents are completely visible.

- File folders make simple small game boards. Game pieces can be put into a library book-type pocket and adhered directly to the folder or into a Ziploc® bag attached to the folder with a paper fastener.

• Half gallon cardboard milk cartons are a valuable resource. With a few alterations two cartons will provide a sturdy small box, complete with a lid that absolutely will not fall off. After washing

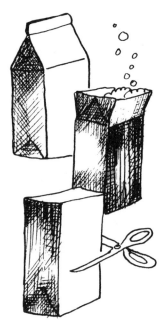

and drying the cartons thoroughly, cut off the tops so that all lateral sides are identical. One carton is the top and one is the bottom. Because each is the same size, the container is somewhat expandable to accomodate contents. The outside surfaces of these containers can be used to post examples and directions for an activity. A box containing crayon stubs, for example, might have examples of art projects requiring crayon stubs (crayon rubs, crayon resist, etc.) with specific directions for each activity on the surfaces. These boxes are unique in that there are always 2 in 1 and they will hold liquids as well as solids should the need arise.

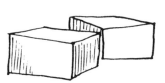

• Pringle cans are another very versatile resource and are readily available. These containers provide handy storage for supplies as well as ideal storage for board games which have been somewhat adapted. Specific procedures for making learning games more transportable are given in greater detail in the "Backpack Back-Up" section.

Summary

One of the distinct benefits in substitute teaching is the exposure to a variety of classroom environments. Such experiences lend themselves well to professional development and the collection of new ideas. As a substitute teacher absorbs new ideas and begins to develop a "survival kit," he or she will eventually outgrow and/or modify a single container. It will then become necessary to evaluate the kit's contents on a daily basis depending on preferences and assignments.

As it has already been stated, a substitute's "survival kit" should be very personal to accomodate style and territory. It must be emphasized that the suggestions offered here are intended merely as launching pads for individual strengths and creativity. Such an attitude will allow for maximum success and professional growth.

TRAIL BLAZING

Initial contacts between you and your students can be critical. Being able to associate names and faces as soon as possible is to everyone's advantage. Name tags or desk markers are not nearly as effective as really getting to know your new charges. The following activities may be helpful as you strive to "blaze such trails." Some of the suggested activities are used only at the beginning of the day but several can be used throughout the day, as needed or desired.

Get Acquainted Bingo

This activity is very effective if introduced with strong emphasis on the need for student cooperation to guarantee its success. An important part of the introduction is creating an awareness that the class has two options: standard roll call procedure versus a more interesting approach. It must also be made clear that student behavior and cooperation are key determinants in the choice. Such an introduction clearly puts the responsibility for success or failure upon the students.

Each student receives a game grid and must collect autographs from classmates to fill the page. Setting a short time limit (2-3 minutes) for this activity is highly recommended. At the same time autographs are being collected, a complete class list must be cut into individual strips representing each student. As numbers would be called for regular Bingo, so names are drawn and called. Players cover name squares as they are called. Five names covered in a row, horizontally, vertically or diagonally, constitutes a "win." Small prizes or privileges may be awarded to winners.

GET ACQUAINTED BINGO

- SIGN YOUR OWN NAME IN THE CENTER SPACE.

- ASK ANYONE IN THE ROOM TO SIGN THEIR NAME IN A SPACE.

- WHEN YOUR SPACES ARE ALL FILLED, YOU ARE READY TO PLAY.

- WHEN NAMES ARE CALLED, COVER THE AUTOGRAPHS WHICH MATCH WITH A MARKER.

- WHEN YOU HAVE 5 NAMES IN A ROW, HORIZONTALLY, VERTICALLY, OR DIAGONALLY, CALL OUT *BINGO* - YOU ARE A WINNER!

Butter Introductions

On a day when you have enough advance notice, you may like to try bringing in a quart size non-breakable container, ½ pint of whipping cream, food coloring, crackers, napkins, and a knife for this activity. The whipping cream should be put into the container with the lid on securely. The container is passed from child to child who "churns" it by shaking it up and down about ten times. While "churning," the children should introduce and/or describe themselves. Primary graders like to make a quick introduction and then count the shakes out loud in a chant. The butter can then be colored according to the mood or occasion and served on crackers for a snack break.

Executive Name Tags

Commercial name tags such as those given to executives at convention time seem to impress elementary age "VIP'S." A one time investment in the plastic, pin-backed, card holders eliminates the need for using straight pins or safety pins. Many students enjoy giving themselves executive titles below their own real name. In addition, they may be encouraged to design logos to accompany their titles. A variation would be for students to do their names in interesting shapes or colors which would give clues as to their hobbies, interests, or mood. Calling in the name tags individually from the class list at the end of the day insures their recovery and a smooth dismissal. The decorated cards may be returned to the students or may be kept for a "return engagement." Many students seem to really appreciate the substitute teacher also wearing a name tag.

"Me Bags"

Standard lunch sacks can be a very useful part of your "survival kit." A not-so-common, very popular use is for "Me Bags." Using magazines, crayons, scissors, index cards, and glue with a lunch bag, students should decorate the outside of their bags with cuttings, drawings, words and phrases which show obvious personal traits. Inside each bag, students place cards upon which they have written or drawn a description of a personal characteristic or quality which is not so obvious and which they would like to share. The bags may be shared verbally or may be hung for display at the end of the day. This activity can be introduced early in the day and worked on as individual schedules dictate. This is often a very revealing activity to those participating; perhaps especially so for the returning classroom teacher.

Fantastic Fish

For the younger students who might not be able to do a satisfying job on "executive" name tags, you may wish to cut "fantastic fish." With a little practice you will be able to cut free-form fish name tags.

The last cut of one fish becomes the first cut of the next fish. Students enjoy watching this process and recognizing the emerging fish particularly if they have not been told what to expect in advance. The cut fish are to be distributed throughout the class--two to each student.

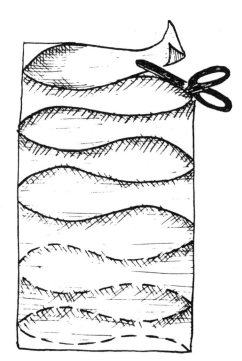

Students are asked to print their names clearly on one of their two fish for use as a name tag. In working with kindergarteners, you may wish to print the names on each fish in advance from a class list. Students identify their own name tags as they enter the classroom. Unclaimed name tags are a possible indication of absentees.

The second fish each student receives may be decorated to reflect the multitude of varieties of fish that exist. Students are then invited to affix their creations to a lake or river environment outlined on large roll paper or on the chalkboard. Students usually delight in enlarging upon the activity so as to create an entire underwater mural by adding sea weed, shells, sunken ships and the like.

Coded Messages

9 ● 1-13 ● 7-12-1-4 ● 20-15 ● 2-5 ● 8-5-18-5!

9-20 ● 9-19 ● 7-15-15-4 ● 20-15 ● 13-5-5-20

YOU!

23-9-20-8 ● 25-15-21-18 ● 8-5-12-16, ●

9-20 ● 23-9-12-12 ● 2-5 ● 1 ● 7-18-5-1-20 ●

4-1-25! *

A neat way to create immediate interest is by using a coded greeting. A set of 30-35 individualized messages on index cards may be developed. If they are laminated, they will last longer and students may decode the messages directly onto each card with crayon or grease pencil. You may wish to simply post a single message for the entire class to solve on the chalkboard. Morse Code, Braille, the International Flag Code or the simple process of substituting numerals for letters in the alphabet are several of many possible code sources. Students may be invited to end the day by sending *you* a coded message.

* You can figure it out! ● separates words

Personal Coat of Arms

This idea comes from Sidney Simon & Associates and the Values Clarification movement.[1] It can be started early in the day and is likely to be something the students will want to work on throughout the day in their spare time. This activity usually proves interesting not only to you and students, but also to the returning teacher and parents. The activity can be done on a ditto using crayons and markers, or on heavier paper with magazine collages, watercolors, as possible media. Introducing the activity with a brief discussion and pictures of coats of arms increases the student's appreciation and knowledge of the historical roots involved. A choice of possible topic headings such as listed below provides assistance and variation for your students who wish to determine their own categories:

My Favorite Book

What Scares Me

What Tickles Me

Things That Make Me Laugh

My Secret Wish

If I Were A Millionaire...

My Gift To The World

What Makes A Friend

Things That "Bug" Me

Hopes For The Future

My Favorite Relative

Things I Appreciate

---

[1] Simon, Sidney B., *Values Clarification: A Handbook of Practical Strategies for Teachers and Students*, Hart Publishing Company, New York, 1972.

My Personal Coat of Arms

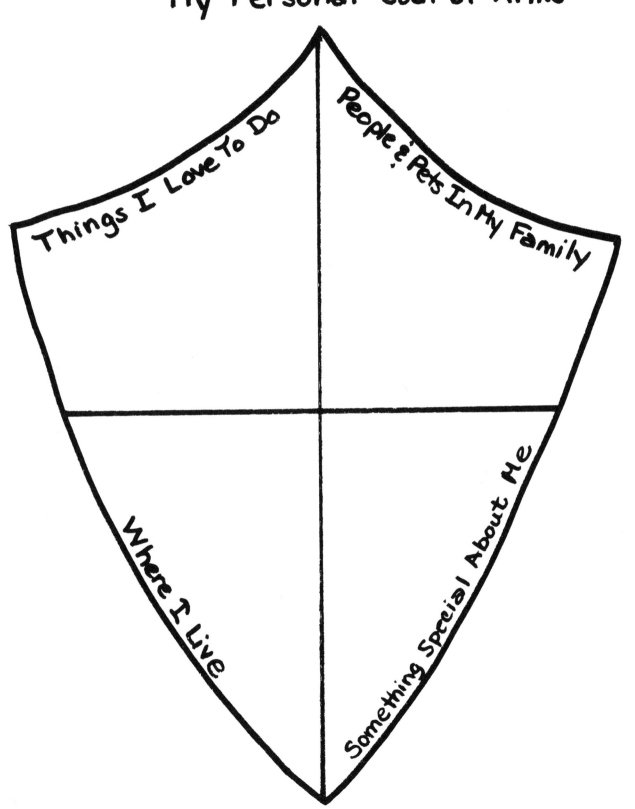

Sequence Games

The possibilities for the use of sequence cards are unlimited. They are useful in developing both thinking and listening skills. Sequence tasks can require reading and following written directions or can be executed solely with picture clues. Such activities are also a natural springboard into limited but enjoyable creative dramatics.

Basically, sequence decks are unnumbered cards that contain instructions which hinge one upon the other and must be performed in correct sequence. "When you hear someone say ———, you must say ———" is an example of a simple way to have the group either tell a story or create some nonsense pattern.

Some of the most entertaining sets of sequence cards use only picture clues. The picture at the top of the card cues the person who must follow. Using pantomime gestures only, the audience must guess what picture is being acted out and whether or not the pantomime represents the illustration at the top of their cards. The student who can link the pantomime to the top picture on the card being held must then pantomime what is pictured at the bottom of the card.

It has been helpful in the past to color in the top or bottom on each card to assist students in discriminating between what to watch for and what to pantomime.

Students also enjoy creating sets of sequence cards. For picture cards, a double set of picture clues is required and one such set has been included here for your convenience.

Matt Likes Mushrooms--Jason Likes Junkfood

This get-acquainted game can go by any name. Using the unusual names of class members in the introduction *seems* to stimulate class interest. The activity expedites name recognition, provides fun for students, and also serves as reinforcement for various grade-level concepts such as initial letter sounds in words. To play the game, individuals must say their name in conjunction with foods that start with the same letters as their names. As the game progresses, individuals must repeat what has already been said by other class members and then "tack on" their own contributions. Students need only recall the food item. The substitute teacher needs to recall both names and related foods. If you are in the mood for a personal challenge, take the last turn. Such a position seems to intensify your association skills and a successful recitation delights the class.

1. I am tall
2. I love pizza
3. I am double-jointed

Mystery Persons Board

One ink pad and a 3" by 5" lined index card for each student are all that is required for this very well received activity. A "chief detective" may be appointed to fingerprint each class member. Once fingerprinted, students write three statements about themselves under the fingerprint and then print their names on the *back* side of the card. All this is done in strict secrecy. The cards are then collected, numbered, and put on display. Throughout the day students may study the cards and attempt to identify the "Mystery Persons" by using the information given on the front side of each card. At day's end students should record the results of their sleuthing on a numbered sheet which corresponds to the numbers assigned to each fingerprint. Plenty of time should be allowed to share the results. A prize might be awarded to the student who correctly identifies the greatest number of classmates.

BACK PACK
BACK-UP

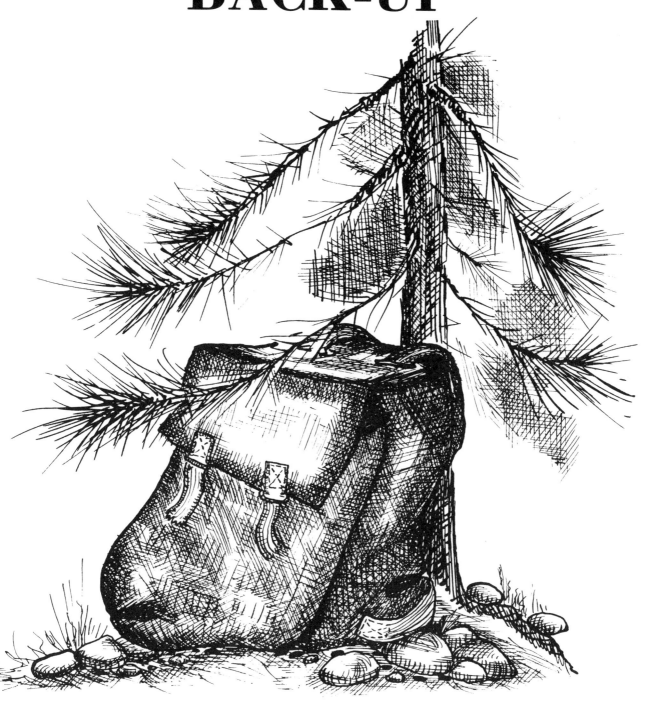

Because the substitute teacher must necessarily be highly adaptable, so too must be the "back up" materials and activities you bring along.

Ideal activities for "back up" are adaptable to a variety of grade levels and subject matter. The best activities are those which are simple but which have potential for expansion in terms of time and complexity.

The *cost* and *space* required to provide activities such as described here for your survival kit are both small--commensurate with a typical substitute teacher's needs and resources.

Creative Cards

Sets of 3" x 5" index cards on which magazine cuts have been glued are simple to make and provide an unlimited resource for activities. Your students will enjoy designing and using such cards. Very often the students will also have excellent suggestions for their use. The picture cards can be used to stimulate creative writing, dramatics, music or poetry. Several sets of cards can be easily kept in your "survival kit." Sets may be organized by theme or category. Several examples of how they may be used are listed below. Your imagination linked with the creativity of your students will take you far beyond this meager list.

• Have students pretend they are the item pictured on the card they receive. Request that they write an entry for that object's "diary."

Example:

"Dear Diary,
    I loved living underground in cool dirt. Today I was hauled away from my happy home, skinned alive, cut into strips, and then plunged into a boiling swimming pool. My only satisfaction was that all the kids loved me--or was it just the ketchup?"

(A Plate of French Fries)

If students are required to guess the identity of each "diary's" author, it motivates them to write more creatively and for more effective communication. Such sharing also provides stimulating classroom discussion.

Writing "diary" entries from a set of cards showing occupations is also a favorite which helps students share and explore their perceptions of the possible worlds of work.

• Another very popular activity, which also serves as an effective tool for teaching basic letter writing skills, requires each student to pretend that the item pictured on the card has been received as a gift for which a "thank you" note must be written. As in real life, this can be a challenge if the gift is not exactly what was expected or needed! The completed "thank yous" are often riotous and usually clever!

• The cards can also be used effectively for small group dramatics and role playing if each group is simply given a card with the request to make a story or commercial centering upon the item or person pictured.

Mystery Box

Every class loves a mystery! Using one of the milk carton cubes, as described earlier, place any little item inside without the students knowing its identity. The students must guess the contents of this "mystery box" by a combination of teacher-given clues and the process of indirect reasoning.

This can be a simple five minute "time filler" or an extended exercise in problem solving depending on your needs or inclination. A simple way to start is to let the class have an unlimited number of guesses to identify an object which they know has been taken from their normal environment. After the students have manipulated the "mystery box" in any way, except by actually opening it, they may ask questions which require only a "yes" or "no" answer. Individual guesses or some group consensus may be presented about the "mystery box" contents. Small prizes may be awarded to "winners." The activity may then be concluded or enlarged upon to further challenge the students' abilities.

Rope Tricks

Contrary to popular student expectations, a piece of rope (jump-rope length) in a substitute's "survival kit" is not intended for tying up students who do not behave! However, there are a few of us who may have been sorely tempted!

By way of introduction, the students are asked to study and comment upon the general properties of the rope. They are given the "power" to change it into anything they desire, providing it retains the general properties which have been listed. For example, the rope could represent a river or a fishing worm. It could be a belt or a dog leash. Using the rope as the only prop,

students pantomime its use or identity. The student who correctly guesses from the pantomime clues becomes the next performer. Other common objects may be used in a similar fashion.

Use of this rope as a jump rope is also a possible way to reward a deserving student. One substitute teacher reportedly used her rope to tie a stubborn icy car door closed one winter. Another substitute teacher used the ruler in her "survival kit" as a much needed window scraper that same winter. Although your "survival kit" may not solve all your problems; you may find it solves some *unexpected* problems!

Attribute Games

Similarities and differences between items are the foundation for a whole host of activities. Being able to identify the attributes which make objects either alike or not alike is a basic thinking skill which is fun to develop. Collections of similar items which are also different might include sets of paper cups, napkins, buttons, round things, etc. For example, a button collection might be distributed one per student throughout a class. The students could be asked to move into groups with similar attributes then explaining the attribute by which they have chosen to organize--such as color, size, or number of holes. If students are then asked several times to disband and re-group on the basis of a different attribute, they will discover a full range of similarities and differences.

Another way to use such collections would be to distribute a collection among class members. Students are asked to work with a partner to make lists of similarities and differences between their assigned items based upon their respective attributes.

Anything from baseball cards to candy bar wrappers may be used in such explorations and the possibilities for activities are limited only by your imagination!

Arrow Stories

Storytelling takes on new dimensions if there is an opportunity for audience participation. Student made sound effects spice up a story considerably and also promote student listening skills. After selecting or creating a story with lots of possibilities for sound effects, create an "arrow," which relates to the story, for volume control. The total group may make all the sounds or individuals may be assigned a specific response to be given when a

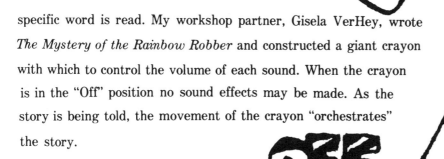

specific word is read. My workshop partner, Gisela VerHey, wrote *The Mystery of the Rainbow Robber* and constructed a giant crayon with which to control the volume of each sound. When the crayon is in the "Off" position no sound effects may be made. As the story is being told, the movement of the crayon "orchestrates" the story.

A set of "slipcovers" for an eighteen inch ruler can be designed for a whole collection of "arrow" stories. A candy cane arrow might be used at Christmas time with a story such as *The Night Before Christmas.*

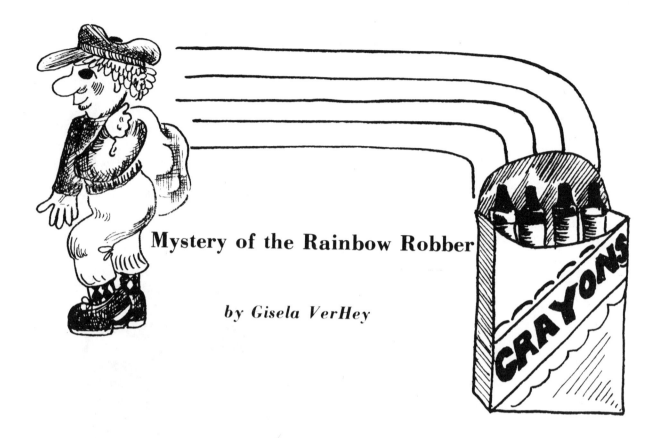

Mystery of the Rainbow Robber

by Gisela VerHey

Tony was so proud of his new box of crayons. He had saved all of his pennies and when he'd had enough, his dad took him to the corner store so he could buy them all by himself. He was glad he had them, too, because it was such a rainy day that he couldn't go out. He was lying on the floor with a big pad of paper, looking at his crayons naming all the colors: red, yellow, blue, black, green, brown, purple, and orange. The TV was on, *playing a little soft music.* Tony was too interested in his colors to listen, but suddenly a newsman interrupted the program. "Attention, everyone! The rainbow robber struck again this morning. He is busy taking everything red that he can see. I repeat. Protect all of your red items." Tony jumped up and looked for his *red wagon with the squeaking wheels.* It was gone! He looked for his *red fire engine with the real siren.* Gone, too! He ran to the drawer where he saved his icky sticky red sucker. Oh dear! He looked out the window and his friend the *redheaded woodpecker was not pecking the telephone pole.* Suddenly Tony remembered his crayons and ran back to the living room. It was a close call, but his red crayon was still there. He decided that he would never put them down. He even put them under his pillow when he went to sleep at night.

It was a good thing he did, because the next day everything green was gone. No more *frogs, croaking in the pond.* No more *green leaves whispering in the wind.* No more green *7-Up bottles full of bubbly gurgly fizzles.* But Tony still had his green crayon, tight in his hand or under his pillow when he

*Reprinted with permission of author.

went to sleep at night.

The next day there were no *blue cars whizzing down the highway*. There were no *blue jays scolding in the trees*. There were no *blue lakes splashing against the shore*. But Tony still had all of his crayons when the *alarm clock rang each morning*.

The Rainbow Robber took all of the *yellow chicks that peeped in the barnyard*. Then he took the *yellow ducklings swimming on the pond*. He took every yellow thing he could find except the sun and that was too hot.

The next day there were no big *orange trucks rumbling down the highway...no juicy slurpy oranges to eat. No crunchy orange carrots for rabbits to crunch*.

Then he took the *brown dogs*, and the *brown cows*, and the *splishy splashy mud puddles, so good for stomping in*. He took all the big *black cats* and he captured every last one of the *big black giant thunderclouds*.

Soon there was no color left but purple in the world outside Tony's window. He began to miss the many colors that were stolen by the Rainbow Robber, but he still had all of his crayons, and he was beginning to worry about what would happen when the robber had taken all of the colors and might try to trick him out of his crayons. He decided on a plan. Purple was the next color to be stolen so Tony carefully *filled a glass with purple grape juice*.

He put it in the middle of the kitchen table and then he hid behind a curtain. The house was very quiet now with all of the colorful things missing. Suddenly Tony heard *tiny footsteps*...and there was the Rainbow Robber! Why he was no bigger than an elf. Tony reached out quickly and grabbed him with

one hand. (He was holding his box of crayons with the other hand.) The Rainbow Robber *screeched a high-pitched scream.* "Let me go!" he screamed. But Tony told him to be quiet. When he finally stopped struggling, Tony asked him what he was going to do with all of the colors he had taken. "Well," said the tiny fellow, "I wanted to get a job with Jack Frost, painting leaves. Or maybe with Santa, painting the toys. So I decided that the first thing I would need would be all the colors of the rainbow and I began to collect them because they were so beautiful!" "Well, you've made a mess of things," said Tony. "The world is pretty dreary without colors. I have an idea. If I can get you a box of crayons like mine, you can bring back all of the other colors because you can make anything you want with a box of new crayons. Look, I'll show you."

And Tony made a *big green frog,* and a *fuzzy yellow duckling,* and a *bright red fire engine.* The little elf couldn't believe his eyes. He *clapped his hands with glee.* "Why one box of crayons can do everything and it's alot easier than taking care of so many noisy things. I have some pennies saved up. Could you get me a box?" "Sure," said Tony...and he did. Now on rainy days, you can see Tony and his new little friend *drawing all kinds of colorful noisy pictures.* They are *laughing at all the fun they are having...*And the *blue jays are back in the trees, and the woodpeckers are pecking at the telephone poles, and the green leaves are rustling in the trees...*just like they always were.

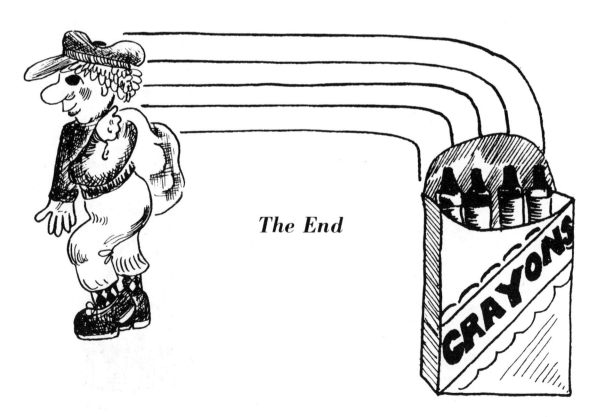

The End

Fabric Fabrications

A collection of fabric swatches in a variety of colors and textures can provide a valuable back-up resource for your "survival kit." The swatches lend themselves well to "instant" creative dramatics or creative writing. The attributes of each particular swatch may suggest a character or story line to an individual or a small group may work with many swatches to develop a short play.

Another way to use fabric swatches would be for students to write a story or poems incorporating the characteristics of the swatch assigned to them so that the rest of the class could guess from which fabric swatch their stories have originated.

Blank Books

Blank Books are simply small "books" consisting of blank pages stapled inside a "cover" of construction paper, cardboard, or wallpaper. A variety of sizes and covers is provocative to contributing authors, artists, and potential readers alike. Blank Books are an exciting way to provide for those students who have extra time on their hands. The substitute teacher may choose to act as a "publisher" in search of a specific type of book to "publish" or as a librarian seeking to build a mobile library for use between school buildings or even between school districts.

Students may create picture books, diaries, novels, or puzzle books to be taken home or to be donated to the "Sub's Roving Library" for sharing with other students with whom the substitute teacher comes into contact. In one case a "chain" adventure story which began in a third grade class in one building and was completed by a sixth grade class in another school district seven teaching assignments later, became a veritable "best seller!"

Egg Carton Mancala

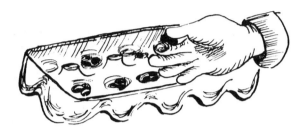

Sets of single dozen styrofoam egg cartons can be used in a variety of ways if kept handy in your "survival kit." By far the most popular use is for a game called "Mancala."

Mancala is said to have originated in Africa over 3,500 years ago. It was played by tribes in every part of Africa, and is often called "The African Stone Game." The natives played this game by scooping out pits in the sand and small stones were used for playing pieces.

The game is popular because it is simple to learn yet always different and intellectually stimulating for all ages. The complexity of the game depends entirely upon the level of strategy sophistication of the two players.

The rules for this game are not the same the world over. One basic game and some variations are suggested in these rules. Provided both players are agreeable, any number of rule modifications can be made to make the game even more interesting and challenging.

The Rules

1. Two players sit opposite each other with an egg carton between them. The six little "pits" directly in front of each player belong to that player. The area to the right of the six little pits which is marked with a circle is each player's "cala." It is helpful to identify this area with a butter tub or in some other way for young children and most beginners.

2. Three "stones" (pebbles, navy beans, macaroni, buttons - some type of counter) are placed into each pit. The object of the game is to end up with more "stones" in your "cala" than your opponent has in the other "cala."

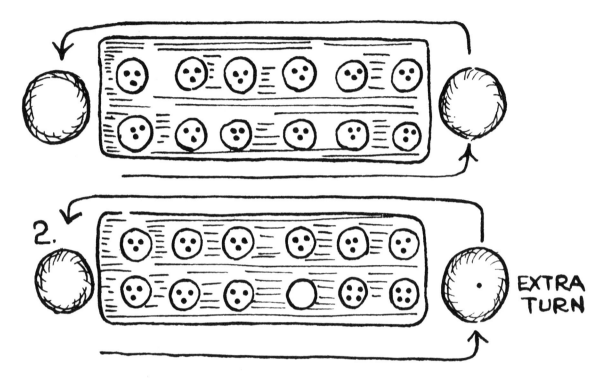

3. The first player picks up all the stones in any one of the six pits which belong to that player and distributes them one at a time from left to right around the carton. During this process players will always deposit a stone in their own "calas" but never in their opponent's "calas." By depositing the *last* stone of the group picked up at the beginning of their turns in their own "calas," players may earn an additional turn. Players may continue to play as long as the last stone in a turn is placed in their own "cala."

4. The game ends when either player empties their own row of six little "pits." However, the player who does this first does not necessarily win unless that player also has a greater number of stones in the "cala" to the player's right side.

For Variation students may choose to play beginning with four stones in each pit.

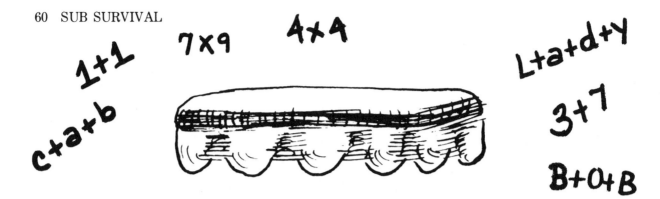

This same type of egg carton may also be used for word or number "scrambles" by simply labeling the bottom of each depression with numbers or letters. For "Word Scramble," several stones are placed in the carton. The carton is closed and students shake or "scramble" the "eggs." When the carton is opened students attempt to make words using the letters which have been covered by stones as a result of the shaking process. For "number scramble," the numbers which have been covered may be used as the basis for computation in any of the four basic number operations: addition, subtraction, multiplication, or division.

Teaching Place Value

"All Hands on Deck"

Following are four activities which require only a deck of cards, pencil, and paper. Students usually enjoy these activities and would probably be quite surprised to know that by playing this game they are receiving valuable experience with basic place value concepts.

Place Value Solitaire or Quartet

Use all the cards in the deck numbered 1-9. Each player (1-4) receives one suit of the cards numbered 1-9. Each player also needs paper and pencil. Write all the three digit numbers you can make from these cards and then order them from lowest to highest. Do this two more times. Students may compare their results with other players or show the substitute teacher their work.

Greatest, Least, and In-Between

Three students may play this game. Three suits of cards are needed for this game. Do not use the face cards. Each player draws 3 cards and arranges the cards without showing other players to form a numeral. Decide if your numeral is greatest, least, or in-between. Each player tells what he predicts his numeral will be and displays his cards. A point is earned for each correct prediction and the winner is the person who first accumulates 10 points.

★★★★ Starshine ★★★★

All the cards in the deck numbered 1-9 are shuffled. As many as 30 students may play. Each player needs paper and pencil or copies of the pattern below to work with. The leader calls one number at a time to make the largest number possible. The person who gets the largest number may put a star by line A. Play continues until one or all players earns four stars.

Example: ★ A) __9__ __6__ __4__ __2__ __1__

B) ___ ___ ___ ___ ___

C) ___ ___ ___ ___ ___ and so on

Little Boxes

Use all the cards of one suit in the deck numbered 1-9. Shuffle the cards. The leader draws 7 cards one at a time and 2-30 players place the number as it is called in a box on the game sheet. When the leader directs players to put (+) in the operation circle, the winner is the player with the highest total. Play continues until one player has won five times or it seems appropriate to quit. The operation sign can be changed to minus (-). Winners can be persons with the least or the greatest sum OR least or greatest difference. Although luck plays a part in winning this game, skill is also necessary.

Little Boxes Game Sheet

Math Scavenger Hunt

A math scavenger hunt is simple to set up and is an interesting way to challenge students who complete their required work early. The activity can also be used as a total group activity if that is more desirable.

A math scavenger hunt can be designed so as to include mapping and graphing activities, measurement skills, and library research. The physical perimeter of the hunt can range from the confines of an individual student's desk to use of the school library and other areas of the building site. The purpose of the hunt can be to give correct responses to each of a series of questions or the individual answers can be mathematically hinged together to lead toward a single amount as in the example below. The chances for error are greater when such a "bottom line" is the student's goal because not only must the individual responses be correct but they must also be correctly processed as well--a bit more challenging.

You may wish to develop several math scavenger hunts in order to fit different school environments and skill levels or you may want to create a fill-in-the-blanks master ditto which can be personalized for each class or individual.

A Math Scavenger Hunt for YOU!

Record your age on line 1.   1. —————

Add the number of letters in your teacher's last name and record the sum on line 2.   2. —————

Add the number of years that Abraham Lincoln served as President of the United States. Record the sum on line 3.   3. —————

Multiply what you have on line three by the number of pecks there are in one bushel. Record the amount on line 4.   4. —————

Subtract the number of inches that your teacher's desk is tall from the amount on line four. Record the difference on line 5.   5. —————

Divide the amount on line five by the number of times the Vice President of the United States has taken over as President of the United States. Record that amount on line 6.   6. —————

Add the number of students who belong in this class to the figure on line six. Record that sum on line 7.   7. —————

Subtract the number of years in a decade from the amount of line seven. Record the difference on line 8.   8. —————

Add the year that World War II ended to the figure on line eight. Record the sum on line 9.

9. ——————

Divide the amount on line nine by the number of centimeters in one meter. Record this final figure on line 10.

10. ——————

"American Graph-itti"

Simple graphing activities are easy to introduce with very enjoyable end results. A set of activity cards composed of surveying and graphing tasks fits easily into any "survival kit" and can be used in wide variety of situations. Students delight in such individualized assignments and love to compare their completed work.

Examples of Possible Activity Cards:

- Pick a paragraph from the newspaper. Pick 10 of your favorite letters from the alphabet. Tally and graph how many times each letter appears in the paragraph.

  What letter in the alphabet do you think is used most frequently? How could you prove your answer?

- Survey, tally, and graph the birthdays in your classroom.

- Throw a pair of dice 100 times. Record the value of each throw. Graph your results.

• Choose a page in your reading book. Count and record the number of one letter words on the page. Do the same for words with 2, 3, 4, 5 or 6 letters. Make a graph to show your results.

• Survey, tally, and graph one of these:

  * color of socks worn in this classroom
  * hair colors of classroom members
  * favorite foods of classroom members
  * family size of classroom members
  * lunch contents of classroom members

• Look out a window where there is traffic moving. Watch and tally for 5 minutes. Make a graph to show the kinds and numbers of vehicles which pass by.

• How do you use your time? Make graphs to show how you use your time.

  * at school
  * at home
  * total time

M-M-M-M Good Math

These graphing activities provide an excellent incentive for completing required work and perhaps lend credence to the somewhat adjusted adage that the "best way to a kid's heart is through the stomach!"

- *The dentists probably love this one!*

  * Work with a friend.
  * Take a package of Lifesavers® or M&M's®.
  * "Guess-timate" how many of each color will be in the package.
  * Check out your predictions.
  * Make a picture graph to share your results with the class.
  * Split the candy fairly between you. How many each? Any left-overs?

- *This activity is the result of a watermelon surplus in one substitute teacher's garden!*

  * Take a slice of watermelon.
  * Before sinking your teeth into it, "guess-timate" how many seeds your piece will have. Record the number.
  * Eat and tally.
  * Graph your total on the class graph.
  * Is there any correlation between the number of seeds and a certain part of the melon? Can that be shown on the graph?

- Doing this activity at the end of the day is an ideal way to reward a class that is "Super for the Sub."

  * Draw a target such as would be found on a dartboard on an old tablecloth or bed sheet. Put a popcorn popper in the "bullseye" spot.
  * Pop a batch of corn with the lid off.
  * Station students around the perimeter of the target to note where the various puffs of corn land.
  * Graph the results.
  * Pop a second batch for munching and crunching!

Wastebasket Archaeology

"One person's junk is another person's treasure" is very true for this activity. All that is required for Wastebasket Archaeology is a little cooperation and a little "junk" from a neighboring classroom - both of which are not that difficult to obtain. The "junk" which is needed comes in the form of another classroom's wastebasket. The cooperation needed is in the form of "feedback" from the very class who accumulated the "junk."

After borrowing a wastebasket which has been the recipient of a large portion of the day's cast-offs, divide the class into "dig teams." Each "dig team" should examine a layer of trash and make hypothesis about events which may be linked to each "find." Each team may wish to make other tentative statements about the participating class on the basis of its discoveries.

Unlike official archaeologists who must base their suppositions upon indirect evidence, your classroom archaeologists will have the opportunity to check out their hypothesis with the class from which the evidence originated. Such feedback serves as a way to develop thinking skills in a manner which is also alot of fun.

Portable

Learning Centers

A portable learning center based on a theme or subject area can be very useful and is much appreciated by many students. Such a learning center can be supplemental or if necessary can be a good foundation for the day's activities.

One of the most interesting and motivating kinds of centers to tote along is one based upon a children's book. It can focus in on a small picture book which can be introduced to a class as they begin to work in the center or the center can be based upon a classic such as *Charlotte's Web* with which most classes will be familiar. Other such lengthy books might also be used if the length of the substitute teacher's assignment allows for it.

A *Charlotte's Web Center* could include a large variety of activities in all subject areas. One such center includes: a computation game called *Arachnid*, a set of Wilburs (the pig who is a main character in the story) with words from the story which need to be alphabetized, and reaction cards for pertinent quotes from the story to which students react in terms of what has been said. These are just a few examples. The only limit to what can be done is in terms of your imagination and the amount of energy you are willing to invest.

Straw Weaving

Making belts, bracelets, bookmarks, and headbands from yarn is a simple and rewarding project which can be enjoyed by first through sixth grade students. The basic materials required include a plastic drinking straw and a small ball of yarn (about the size of a golf ball) for each student. One four ounce skein of four ply yarn is enough for about ten students. Yarn which is variegated or several colors of yarn can be used to create an interesting effect.

Even the preparations for this activity can be used to your advantage and provide an excellent opportunity to harness student resources while building anticipation for the day's events. Rather than using your precious time to make the necessary yarn balls, let the students "get the ball rolling." While routine organizational kinds of tasks are being taken care of early in the day, employ two students to roll the skein of yarn into one large ball. This large ball of yarn can then be passed on to another student who is directed to roll it into two yarn balls of equal size. The two yarn balls are then passed on to two other students who should again divide the ball they receive into two smaller yarn balls of equal size. The process continues until the yarn balls are down to the size of a golf ball. Purposely not divulging the purpose of these preparations is very provocative, making even the most unwilling student quite curious and interested.

The beauty of this activity lies not only on its simplicity but the high level of student satisfaction with the finished product. Straw weaving has the additional advantage of being easily picked up and put down at any time. It can be a short term project or it can fill many hours depending upon individual interest levels and available time.

Directions for this activity can be given in written form to individual students or small groups who will work independently from the other class members. Materials for as many as ten students can be kept in a milk carton cube as described earlier with the step by step directions printed on the outside surfaces of the container. This can be an interesting challenge to the more capable students who often finish basic requirements early.

This activity may also be introduced to a single student who would in turn teach someone else so that that person could teach another person -- "snowball" fashion -- as individuals are ready to try the project.

Another option would be to do a demonstration with the entire class letting students who later have "free time" come back to the project as their schedules allow.

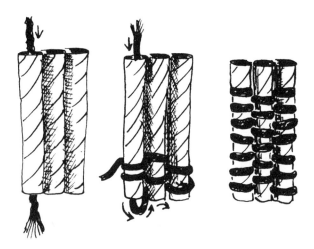

Directions

1. Cut a drinking straw into three equal sections.

2. Thread a length of yarn through each piece of straw. Fold about a half inch of the yarn back along the straw and secure with a small piece of tape.

3. Tie the loose end of the ball of yarn around *one* of the straws.

4. Holding the three straws side-by-side in one hand, use the other hand to wind yarn alternately over and under the three straws.

5. As the straws fill with yarn, slide the woven section carefully down onto the three yarn "tails." To keep the weaving from sliding completely off the "tails," knot the "tails" loosely together about six inches from the end.

6. When the desired length has been woven, remove the straws and tie off the two sets of "tails."

7. Tie the "tails" together to form bracelets or headbands or leave as is for belts and bookmarks. Tassles may be attached for added effect.

Once students have mastered the basic technique they may wish to increase the number of straws to widen the piece being woven.

Cut-Rub-Spatter

Using virtually any kind of paper, a whole host of creations can be cut and used to create murals, get-well cards for the teacher, etc. This basic activity can be used as the foundation for many other art activities as well.

Cut snowflakes, flowers, butterflies, etc. can be placed under a sheet of art paper. By "rubbing" the paper with a crayon a student can make the design magically appear on his paper. The cut may be moved to create an overlapping effect and using a different color of crayon also adds to the artist's own special touch. Cookie cutters may also be used to make templates for crayon rubs.

These cut designs can also be used for spatter painting. A piece of window screen stretched over a cardboard half gallon milk container with one side removed makes a workable "frame." An old toothbrush is the painting tool. Mix a few drops of food coloring with water and dip the brush into the solution. Brush across the screen and small specks of color will fall upon the paper which has been placed in the bottom of the milk carton. To make a design, place a shape cut from newspaper on the paper before spattering. Any pattern or object placed on the paper will remain white and the pattern emerges as the shape is removed. Art activities such as these are very basic but allow for great creativity which will be pleasing to both teacher and student. The finished products can also be used in a variety of ways--wrapping paper, greeting cards, and wall hangings to name just a few.

Happy Holidays

Coping with students who are highly stimulated by holiday excitement can be rather demanding at times. Maintaining a nice collection of holiday activities gives a substitute teacher plenty of ammunition for channeling holiday spirits in a positive direction.

Two very reliable ways to "teach and reach" during such times are shared here. They are very simple--not terribly creative--but usually very successful.

Follow the Directions Holiday Mural

This is a total group project which requires careful reading and execution of directions but also legitimately allows for the physical movement and socialization which children seem to need during such seasons.

The "mural" can be wall size or simply within the 8½" x 11" dimensions of any sheet of paper. A set of directional cards large enough to provide each student with one card must be designed for the various holidays.

On each card, a written direction is printed.

Example:

> In the lower left hand corner, below the Christmas tree, draw a large Christmas package wrapped in green and red paper with a big bow on top. The gift tag should say: "From Santa With Love." Do not draw this Christmas package until someone else has drawn the Christmas tree.

Every child receives a card and the directions may be carried out under the teacher's direction with the whole group working together or by individuals fitting the task into their personal schedules.

The resulting mural can be a real delight and the process can also be a true learning experience.

Compute and Color

Even sixth graders welcome an excuse to color! And students seem a little more eager to do computation if they are also asked to "color" the answer.

Compute and Color math drills are easy to design and easy to correct. Most substitute teachers simply "steal" a picture from a child's coloring book for a Compute and Color answer sheet. The worksheet has fifteen to twenty math problems on it with multiple choice answers each of which is assigned a color. Students compute each problem, choose the correct answer from those listed, and then "color the answer onto the answer sheet in the designated area.

COMPUTE and COLOR

START HERE → Color the space in picture the color of the correct answer.	#1 8×8	#2 5×9	#3 $17 + 29$
	64 green 16 red 72 orange 15 pink	14 red 45 white 56 purple 30 green	45 purple 19 yellow 103 black 46 orange
#4 92×7 99 red 644 white 634 blue 604 orange	#5 $126 + 975$ 1,091 blue 1,101 red 891 white	#6 $900 - 279$ 631 black 779 blue 621 brown	#7 $7\overline{)357}$ 51 purple 5 green 5R2 orange
#8 $10\overline{)20,000}$ 20,000 orange 200 yellow 2,000 purple	#9 19×10 1,900 green 190 red 19,000 black	#10 $3\overline{)22}$ 6 R2 red 7 white 7 R1 orange	#11 16×7 112 blue 102 purple 23 black
#12 $15\overline{)458}$ 4 orange 3 R8 green 3 red	#13 12×12 24 blue 136 yellow 144 green	#14 12×4 46 green 48 red 16 orange	#15 $7\overline{)150}$ 21 R3 red 21 R6 orange 2 R5 blue
#16 $3\overline{)21}$ 7 R5 yellow 7 blue 6 R2 red	#17 $1,000 - 873$ 173 orange 1,873 black 127 red 273 white	#18 14 15 16 $+ 29$ 53 green 54 yellow 74 blue	Good work!

Home-Made Games

A variety of games which teach or reinforce basic concepts and skills can be most helpful in keeping students busy, enthused, and productive. The critical concern for the substitute teacher is to keep the "delivery system" for each game "transportable" enough to justify bringing it along.

Almost any gameboard can be drawn on permanent press fabric with either permanent markers or in liquid embroidery. These "gameboards" can be laundered and are easily packed for any journey. Because the "delivery system" is so compact a variety of games can be taken along at any given time. Gameboards drawn on file folders are also very compact.

One of the nicest aspects of substitute teaching is the number of opportunities there are for exposure to new game ideas which can be incorporated into your "survival kit."

Bottle Band

An 8-pak of screw top throw-away cola bottles provides the basic ingredients for an inexpensive, highly portable and adaptable musical experience for the children with whom you visit. To begin with, tune the bottles by filling them with water from middle C to the C one octave higher. Mark the level of each bottle with a permanent marker so you can quickly refill them at another time. You may also want to make color-coded song sheets. Simple rounds and holiday songs work well. Bottles may be played by tapping or blowing. Children may like to experiment individually during free time or you may want to do this as a class activity. For use with the whole class you may want to make more than one set of bottles. Four sets (32) are usually enough to give each person in an average sized class a bottle to play -- and 4 persons on each note helps eliminate alot of stage fright!

"We've Always Got Rhythm"

Activities based on the age old love of a good rhythm are an ever ready resource for the substitute teacher. The possibilities are unlimited. Here are just two examples of what may be done:

1. To stimulate listening skills, request students to "echo" a rhythm pattern tapped out on a desk top. This can be a teacher directed activity or be done in round-robin fashion. Such echoing can be easily used to fill in "empty" minutes which may occur during the day.

2. Rhythm "stories" can also be tapped out by one person with the rest of the class attempting to identify and verbalize the "plot."

Mystery Seeds

A good way to use those small amount of left-over seeds from last year's garden is to package them in small envelopes. Planting directions and "mystery clues" should be written on the outside of the envelope.

Example:

Planting Directions

Plant these "mystery seeds" about ¼ inch deep in a cup of soil or Vermiculite. Keep soil moist and locate the cup in sunlight. These seeds should germinate in about 21 days.

Mystery Clue

Roses are red
Violets are blue
It's neither of these two!

A small can of Vermiculite or potting soil, the mystery packets, and paper cups can be easily kept in any "survival kit."

"Mystery Seeds" packets can be used as a special reward for an individual student or may simply serve as a special remembrance of your day together. Classes who have enjoyed Arnold Lobel's *Frog and Toad* stories like "The Garden" (found in *Frog and Toad Together*) will particularly enjoy such a parting gift. A substitute teacher who returns to a class on a regular basis may request that a "growth log" be kept.

Ditto File

Many substitute teachers have developed and carry with them a file of ditto masters and/or multiple copies which can be used upon a moment's notice. Such collections include dittoes which reinforce basic skills like subtraction and punctuation or dittoes to be used as part of an enrichment activity. A file folder of blank dittoes is very helpful. Very often you will come across clever dittoes discovered or designed by the regular classroom teacher which you will want to add to your resources.

* These are all well known sayings or phrases made up by students.

* To get you rolling — #4 is a BLACK OVERCOAT

* Good Luck!

1. EZ / i i i i	2. T O U C H	3. MOTH cry cry cry	4. BLACK / COAT
5. TIME TIME	6. Land	7. HURRY ↑	8. ME QUIT
9. LE VEL	10. MAN / BOARD	11. KNEE / LIGHT	12. HE'S/Himself
13. R|E|A|D|I|N|G	14. AGES	15. R R OAD A D	16. O / B.S. M.A. Ph D.
17. what's ↑	18. STAND / I	19. ↓ TOWN	20. CYCLE CYCLE CYCLE

Design a T-Shirt

For the Shirt Gallery

Draw 4 black cats.
Give one white paws.

Draw 1 witch.
Put a wart on her nose.

Draw 6 scarey faces.
Make one with green hair.

Draw 5 ghosts. Put happy
faces on three of them.

Draw 3 orange pumpkins.
Make one frown.

Draw 2 scarecrows.
Dress one in red pants.

Cut these shapes out.

See if you can form
a square □

A GAME FOR TWO

1. You will need fifteen (15) objects. You may use stones or counters. Place them between your partner and yourself.

2. Decide who will have the first go, then take turns to pick up one, two, or three objects.

3. The one who manages to pick up the last item LOSES. Always try to make your partner take it!

4. Play at least 10 games and keep a record like the one below:

    1ˢᵗ game: A B A B A B A
                3 3 1 3 3 1 1

                       Player A Lost!

    2nd game

                  etc.

5. Try to find out if there is any way to guarantee a win if you have first turn — if you have second turn.

MAKE AN ALPHABET ZOO

A B C D E F

G H I J K L

M N O P Q R

S T U V W

X Y Z

Feed Ravenous Ruth . . . .
Anything that starts with "R"

_____   _____

_____   _____

_____   _____

_____   _____

_____   _____

_____   _____

_____   _____

Pick a magazine.

Cut out, Paste and Label:

2 Things that would hold something little:

2 Things that would hold something large:

Something that moves slowly:

Something that moves fast:

Happy Holidays!

How many different words can you make using the letters in this holiday greeting?

_____ _____ _____

_____ _____ _____

_____ _____ _____

_____ _____ _____ _____

_____ _____ _____ _____

_____ _____ _____ _____

_____ _____ _____ _____

_____ _____ _____ _____

_____ _____ _____ _____

_____ _____ _____ _____

_____ _____ _____ _____

The 4 Color Game

Use red, green, blue, yellow crayons.

Color the designs below so that no two areas which touch are the same color.

You may use no more than 4 colors. Use as few as possible.

Compare your work with a friend's work. Can you determine how many different ways each design may be colored and still meet the above requirements?

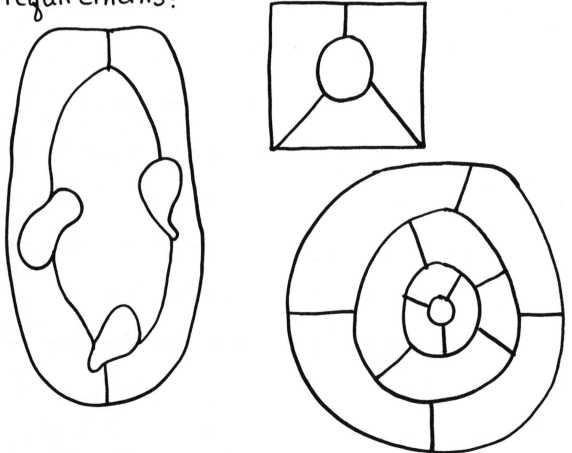

Write your name or any letters from
the alphabet on the grid below.

NAME or LETTERS	FOOD	PLACE	ANIMAL
EXAMPLE D	dog food	Detroit	Deer

"MILK CARTON GEOMETRY"

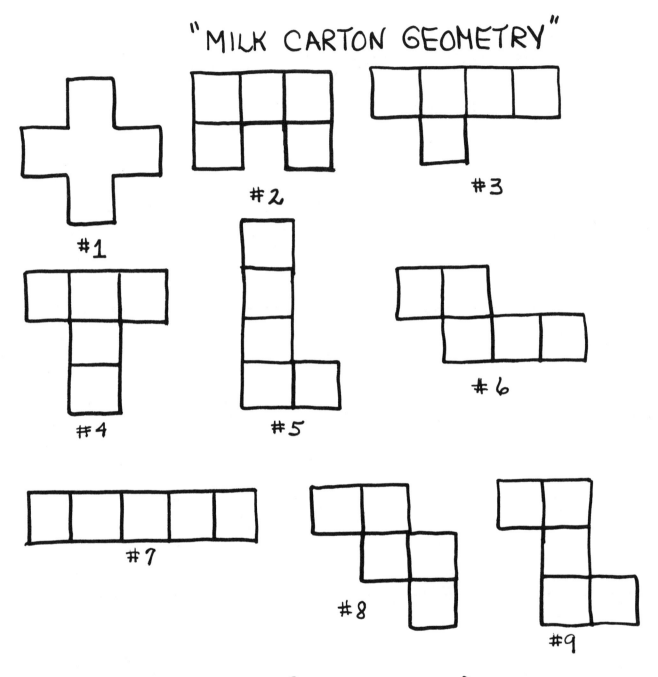

#1

#2

#3

#4

#5

#6

#7

#8

#9

Which of these figures could fold up into a milk carton without a lid?

Using a clean milk carton from the school lunch program— Pick a pattern from those above and cut your carton to match.

Evaluation

Successful substitute teachers are constantly evaluating strategies which *are* or *are not* effective in the classrooms to which they have been assigned. Whether such evaluation is done formally or informally, the students themselves can provide valuable insight to the process if a substitute teacher is willing to listen.

Whatever the evaluation tool, it should have a highly personal but simple design which quickly provides desired information.

The evaluation included here requires the students to access their own role in the successes or failures of the day. This kind of evaluation is a reflection of the belief that the students themselves are also partly responsible for the day's outcome.

Let's Rate the Day

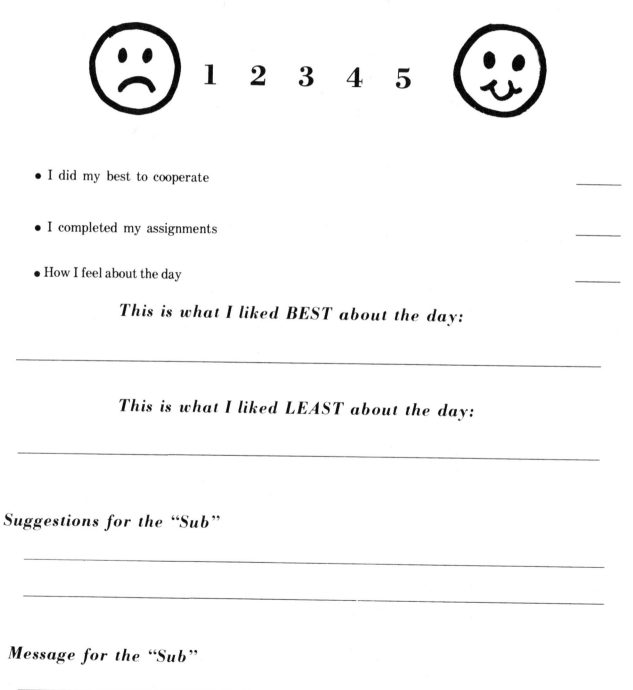

1   2   3   4   5

- I did my best to cooperate   _____

- I completed my assignments   _____

- How I feel about the day   _____

This is what I liked BEST about the day:

_____

This is what I liked LEAST about the day:

_____

Suggestions for the "Sub"

_____

_____

Message for the "Sub"

_____

_____

Hopefully many of the activities listed in "Backpack Back-Up" will be useful or at least inspirational to you. It must be kept in mind, however, that the success of such activities depends to a large extent upon you.

The manner in which activities are introduced is critical and a successful approach often takes time and sensitivity to develop.

Your personal level of enthusiasm is contagious. If these suggested activities do not appeal to you or fit your teaching style, by all means develop something more appropriate.

A substitute teacher who has learned to be highly flexible can better "roll with the punches" and will feel both comfortable and successful. Flexibility is both an attitude and a skill. Substitute teaching experiences can teach you new meanings of the word "flexibility" if approached positively and as yet another learning experience in the course of your professional and personal development.

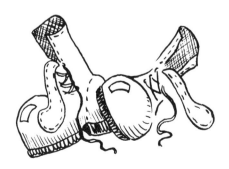

NATURAL RESOURCES

The most important natural resource you have as a substitute teacher is your own creativity and enthusiasm. Your "survival kit" is a reflection of those two qualities plus a small investment of time and money.

A "survival kit" does not have to be very expensive if you take advantage of special prices and are willing to do a little scrounging. For example, instead of ordering your own subscription to a professional magazine, use the copies found in most faculty rooms to augment your idea file.

In general keep your eyes open for little treasures to add to your "survival kit" to make your assignments more adventuresome and rewarding.

Such approaches put together with an attitude of being willing to explore and learn from your substitute teaching experiences is a sure-fire way to feel and be successful in the wilderness.

Sub Survival Bibliography

Freedman, M.K. & Perl, Terri, *A Sourcebook for Subs and Other Teachers*, Addison Wesley, 1974.

Fulk, Virginia Nelson, *The Reading Resource Book: Tried and True Reading Activities for Elementary Students*, Learning Publications, Inc., Holmes Beach, FL, 1984.

Issak, Betty, *Garbage Games*, Learning Works, Inc., Santa Barbara, CA, 1982.

Kaplan, S., *et. al.*, *Change for Children*, Goodyear Publiching Co., Pacific Palisades, CA, 1973.

Lorton, Mary B., *Work Jobs*, Addison Wesley, 1972.

Pavlich, V., and Rosenast, E., *Survival Kit for Substitutes*, Citation Press, New York, NY, 1974.

Pronin, Barbara, *Substitute Teaching: A Handbook for Hassle-free Subbing*, St. Martin Publishers (Macmillan Publishers Ltd.), England, 1983.

Redwine, M.F., *Substitute Teachers' Handbook*, Fearon Publishers, Belmont, CA, 1972.

Sefkow, Paula and Berger, Helen, *All Children Create (Volumes I & II)*, Learning Publications, Inc., Holmes Beach, FL, 1981.

Voight, R.C., *Invitation to Learning*, Acropolis Books Ltd., Washington D.C., 1973.

Weber, Elaine, and Chappa, Janet, *Games that Teach Within Your Reach*, Mott Institute, Michigan State University, 1973.